T0162329

Financial Stability without Central Banks

This publication is based on research that forms part of the Paragon Initiative.

This five-year project will provide a fundamental reassessment of what government should – and should not – do. It will put every area of government activity under the microscope and analyse the failure of current policies.

The project will put forward clear and considered solutions to the UK's problems. It will also identify the areas of government activity that can be put back into the hands of individuals, families, civil society, local government, charities and markets.

The Paragon Initiative will create a blueprint for a better, freer Britain – and provide a clear vision of a new relationship between the state and society.

FINANCIAL STABILITY WITHOUT CENTRAL BANKS

GEORGE SELGIN

with commentaries by

MATHIEU BÉDARD

KEVIN DOWD

Institute of
Economic Affairs

First published in Great Britain in 2017 by
The Institute of Economic Affairs
2 Lord North Street
Westminster
London SW1P 3LB
in association with London Publishing Partnership Ltd
www.londonpublishingpartnership.co.uk

The mission of the Institute of Economic Affairs is to improve understanding
of the fundamental institutions of a free society by analysing and expounding
the role of markets in solving economic and social problems.

A CIP catalogue record for this book is available from the British Library.

ISBN 978-0-255-36752-3

Many IEA publications are translated into languages other
than English or are reprinted. Permission to translate or to reprint
should be sought from the Director General at the address above.

Typeset in Kepler by T&T Productions Ltd
www.tandtproductions.com

Printed and bound in Great Britain by Hobbs the Printers Ltd

CONTENTS

THE AUTHORS

Mathieu Bédard

Mathieu Bédard is an economist at the Montreal Economic Institute. He holds a PhD in economics from Aix-Marseille University, and a master's degree in economic analysis of institutions from Paul Cézanne University. He has published over twenty studies with the Montreal Economic Institute, dozens of op-eds for national newspapers in Canada and Europe, and is regularly on television and radio as an economic news commentator.

Kevin Dowd

Kevin Dowd is Professor of Finance and Economics at Durham University and a member of the Academic Advisory Council of the Institute of Economic Affairs. His books include *New Private Monies – A Bit-Part Player?* (IEA, 2014); *Private Money: The Path to Monetary Stability* (IEA, 1998); *The State and the Monetary System* (Philip Allan, 1989); *Laissez-Faire Banking* (Routledge, 1992); *Competition and Finance: A Reinterpretation of Financial and Monetary Economics* (Macmillan, 1996); and, with Martin Hutchinson, *Alchemists of Loss: How Modern Finance and Government Intervention Crashed the Financial System* (Wiley, 2010).

George Selgin

George Selgin is Director of the Cato Institute's Center for Monetary and Financial Alternatives, a Senior Affiliated Scholar at the Mercatus Center at George Mason University, and Professor Emeritus at the University of Georgia. He is the author of *Money: Free and Unfree* (2017); *Good Money: Birmingham Button Makers, the Royal Mint, and the Beginnings of Modern Coinage* (2008); and the IEA Hobart Paper *Less Than Zero: The Case for a Falling Price Level in a Growing Economy* (1997).

FOREWORD

Following the financial crash of 2008, central banks and financial regulators have accrued many new powers. The consensus following the crash was that commercial banks, unless more tightly controlled, were a potential danger to financial stability and the wider economy. Banks in most developed countries have had structural changes imposed upon them and have had their capital more tightly regulated. There has also been a huge increase in the regulation of the conduct of banks. In addition, central banks have adopted so-called 'macro-prudential' policy instruments which attempt to reduce the supply of credit to particular areas of the economy.

The idea that the crash demonstrates that banks need regulating more tightly is certainly contestable. For example, it is clear that there was very little that central banks and financial regulators did in the 2000s that made the crash less likely or its effects more benign. Indeed, much that they did made things worse. Monetary policymakers in the US held interest rates down and stoked the boom. Many of the approaches to regulation encouraged the development of the kind of financial instruments that many believe were at the heart of the crisis. In addition, especially in the US, the government underwriting of financial risk in a number of areas of the financial system encouraged risk taking and lending to risky counterparties. Central bankers and regulators also did not have unique foresight into the events that would unfold. This should call into question approaches to promoting financial stability that involve more regulatory and central bank control of the financial system. For example, the first sentence of the last Bank of England Financial Stability Report issued before the financial crisis started in the UK read: 'The UK financial system remains highly resilient.' Paul Tucker, head of market operations at the Bank of England said in April 2007: 'So it would seem that there is a good deal to welcome in the greater dispersion of risk made possible by modern instruments, markets and institutions.' They were the very instruments that were at the seat of the crisis (though they did not, as such, cause the crisis) and which were encouraged by regulatory and other interventions, especially in the US.

Given this background, the calls to give financial regulators and central banks more power ring a little hollow.

We might well ask what the alternative is to government regulation if we want a safe financial system. We can try to discover the answer to this question by looking at both history and theory. In this fascinating Hayek Memorial Lecture, George Selgin, an esteemed monetary historian, shows how a system of private banks without a central bank can be and has been self-regulating. He also shows how the considerable instability in the US banking system over a very long period of time has been caused by faulty regulation.

Selgin demonstrates how a system of private banks that is not backed by a central bank keeps the system as a whole stable. If one bank stretches credit too far, it will be reined in by the others before things get out of control in the system as a whole. The banks have a strong incentive to ensure an orderly resolution if a particular bank is facing insolvency or illiquidity.

On the other hand, where the monetary system is controlled by a central bank, if the actions of the central bank lead to too much money and credit creation, the system as a whole can become unstable. Selgin compares the Scottish and Canadian banking systems with their English and US counterparts and draws appropriate lessons. Even before the establishment of the Federal Reserve in the US, the country's banking system was heavily regulated. When considering reform, instead of copying Canada's more lightly regulated and more stable system, which had no central bank, in 1913 the US established a central bank. The evidence strongly indicates that this did not bring about greater financial stability.

Two commentaries on this lecture are also illuminating. The first commentary by Kevin Dowd strongly supports George Selgin's arguments in relation to central banks and the instability of the banking system. However, Dowd is emphatic that a monetary system without central banks needs to be underpinned by a gold standard, which he regards as a tried-and-tested institution at the heart of the success of earlier free-banking systems. Mathieu Bédard looks further at the supposed instability of banking systems without central banks. He finds that the theories suggesting that there are inherent instabilities within the banking system are examples of 'blackboard economics' (as Ronald Coase would have put it) – they might be interesting theories, but they are not borne out in reality.

Overall, this collection is a very important contribution to the debate on the future of banking regulation and of central banks. Despite having a poor record before the financial crisis, financial regulators have had their hands strengthened since the crisis. History and theory suggest that there are alternative approaches.

The views expressed in this monograph are, as in all IEA publications, those of the authors and not those of the Institute (which has no corporate view), its managing trustees, Academic Advisory Council members or senior staff. With some exceptions, such as with the publication of lectures (of which this is one), all IEA monographs are blind peer-reviewed by at least two academics or researchers who are experts in the field.

PHILIP BOOTH
Professor of Finance, Public Policy and Ethics at
St Mary's University, Twickenham, and Senior Academic
Fellow at the Institute of Economic Affairs

September 2017

ACKNOWLEDGEMENT

The IEA thanks CQS for the very generous sponsorship of the 2016 Hayek Memorial Lecture and of this publication.

SUMMARY

- In the late eighteenth and early nineteenth century, Scotland had a stable financial system. Its stability arose from the pressure that private banks, which had the right to issue bank notes, placed on each other to behave prudently.
- Unlike in England, the Scottish banking system had no central bank. If one bank within the system over-stretched, it would quickly find its reserves leaking away to other banks and the less prudent bank would have to restrain its behaviour or face failure.
- In one well-known case – that of the Ayr Bank – a problem did arise in relation to its solvency. It failed and brought down some smaller banks. However, it did not bring the system as a whole down because most banks were able to anticipate its failure and ensure that they were not over-exposed.
- This failure ushered in a century of financial stability in Scotland. The fears of those who believe that a central bank has to stand behind a banking system to prevent systemic failure are not borne out in practice.
- A 'free' banking system without a central bank provides incentives for banks to act with restraint. Their lending policies are, in effect, tied to each other. If one over-reaches, it will be pulled back as others

present notes to and demand reserves from the bank that is lending recklessly. This ensures not only the stability of the system, but also stability of overall spending in the economy.

- Such stability of overall spending does not lead to price stability as many understand it – that is, inflation at or close to zero in each and every year. For example, if the total level of reserves in the banking system is relatively fixed, prices may well drift down as productivity and total output rise. However, there will be no systematic bias towards inflation or instability in total spending.
- A banking system that is backed by a central bank has a tendency towards instability. This is because the creation of money by the central bank can inflate money and credit creation in the banking system as a whole. The mechanism of banks restraining the behaviour of each other is blunted. Financial instability and price instability are likely results.
- The banking system in Scotland was more stable than that in England in the late 1700s and early 1800s. Furthermore, the banking system in Canada was stable relative to that in the US. Canada's banking system evolved in a similar way to that in Scotland.
- The US system did not have a central bank (the Federal Reserve) until the early twentieth century. However, regulation and the control and distortion of the banking system by government, especially during and after the Civil War, was disastrous and led to acute instability. Instead of copying the deregulated

Canadian model, in the early twentieth century, the US decided to create a central bank.

- Since the creation of the Federal Reserve, financial stability has worsened. The pre-Federal Reserve model was itself problematic. However, the history of other countries' banking systems suggests that, whatever the problem was, the solution was not a central bank. Financial stability is more likely in a system without central banks and that is not distorted by misguided regulation.

FIGURES

1 PRICE STABILITY AND FINANCIAL STABILITY WITHOUT CENTRAL BANKS: LESSONS FROM THE PAST FOR THE FUTURE

George Selgin

When I was a young boy, my twin brother and I would play a game with my father called 'the five-line game'. I don't know if this was a game anyone else played, but we did. This game worked as follows. We would scribble five lines on a piece of paper, any kinds of lines or curves and what have you, and we would tell my father that he had to make from these lines, incorporating all of them, a picture of something like an elephant or a dog. The idea was that the picture had to look like the thing we wanted it to look like. All the lines had to be used, and they could not look odd. My father was excellent at this game.

What has that got to do with this talk? Well, the five-line game came to mind when I finally got around to taking a good look at the title that had been assigned to my talk, and I found myself thinking, 'How the heck am I going to turn those words into a good lecture?' I struggled with it. Finally I thought, 'I can talk about this; I think I can make it work. But I'll have to cheat a little bit'.

So, I am going to tell you about financial stability without central banks, sure enough; but I am going to cheat by telling you, not about 'price stability ... without central banks', but about financial stability without price stability! I can't help cheating this way because I do not believe that price stability, as it is normally understood – as a stable price level or absolutely stable rate of inflation – is in fact a desirable thing.

I am going to explain to you how we can have stability – financial stability or macroeconomic stability, if you like – without central banks and also without a stable price level, though still with a price level that behaves in a certain systematic fashion.

Financial stability without central banks

As for financial stability without a central bank, well, it is actually rather easy to explain that this is possible because history shows that it is possible. Geographically closest to where we are today, history has given us a good example in the Scottish banking system, which flourished from roughly the latter part of the eighteenth century until the middle of the nineteenth century, when the UK government started to interfere and ruin it, eventually turning it into the disaster that it has become in recent times.

The Scottish system, unlike the English system, did not rely upon a privileged bank of issue, or what would later come to be known as a central bank. This was due to a sort of benign neglect on the part of Parliament. The Bank of Scotland had received the first charter for a banking and currency business in Scotland. But because it was suspected of being a Jacobite institution, Parliament allowed a rival bank, the *Royal* Bank of Scotland, to be established. That step opened the floodgates to what ultimately became a system of numerous banks, all of which could issue bank notes.

It was because there were many banks of issue, almost entirely free from any sort of government regulation, that Scotland ended up with a notoriously stable financial system. The stability was ultimately due to the pressure that the competing banks of issue exerted upon one another by actively presenting notes of rival banks that they received in the course of a business day to those banks for collection, either directly or indirectly through a clearing house, where clerks would figure out how much each bank owed to other banks.

This mechanism created a discipline that was not unlike the discipline one finds in a chain gang. In a chain gang, the prisoners are chained to one another, but none has to be chained to anything else. That's because none of them can run away without being tripped up by the others, and because it's practically impossible for them to coordinate their steps so as to all run away at once, as any of you who has ever been in a three-legged race can imagine.

What's the analogy? It's that, were any one Scottish bank too aggressive in its lending, it would essentially be trying to run ahead of the other banks. But unless all the banks were somehow acting in unison, the aggressive bank would find more of its notes presented to it at settlement time, without itself receiving a like value of other banks' notes, and it would have to have, or get hold of, reserves to cover its net dues to the rest of the system, or else it would default. In short, no Scottish bank could afford to be too generous in its lending if it wished to avoid being 'tripped up' by losing reserves to other banks in the system.

In fact, early in the history of the Scottish system, there was a very good example of how this discipline worked. The example consisted of the notorious failure, which at least some of you have perhaps heard of, of the so-called Ayr Bank, the formal name of which was Douglas, Heron & Company.

Set up around 1770, the Ayr bank and its various branch offices immediately proceeded to lend money on extremely generous terms to various borrowers, with the express aim of becoming the biggest Scottish bank of issue – and doing so very quickly! In making loans, the Ayr exchanged its own paper notes for borrowers' IOUs. Had the Ayr's borrowers just held on to the notes, things might have gone splendidly. But borrowers like to spend the money they borrow. So the notes soon found their way into the hands of Scotland's other banks; and those banks wasted no time returning them to the Ayr Bank for payment.

As theory would predict, the Ayr Bank was soon being bled by its less aggressive rivals. Eventually, if it didn't change course, they would bleed it dry. But the Ayr tried to put off the inevitable, not by contracting its lending, or by rethinking its overall strategy for success, but by borrowing in London to cover its cash losses. Of course, the Ayr couldn't have kept that up for very long under the best of circumstances. In the event, when its London creditor itself failed, the gig was up. Soon afterwards the Ayr folded, bringing some smaller Scottish banks down with it. The rest, having anticipated the debacle, kept safely out of harm's way.

The eventual result of the Ayr's failure – a failure of what had, in fact, become Scotland's biggest bank, as measured by its total assets at the time of its failure – was that Scotland enjoyed almost a century of complete economic and financial stability. There was, thank goodness, no such thing as 'Too Big To Fail' at the time; and Scotland in any case had no central bank capable of carrying out such a policy. Instead, because of the lesson taught by the Ayr Bank's failure, Scotland entered into a long period of remarkable monetary stability, during which no other bank again dared to behave as the Ayr Bank had.

Now, there is also a more subtle advantage of the 'chain-gang discipline' of a competitive banking system, which has to do with how it stabilises the total amount of spending in the system. As I explained before, if they are to survive, competing banks of issue cannot individually be too generous in their lending; but they cannot *collectively* be too generous either, because that would require that they manage somehow to perfectly coordinate their expansionary policies, so that none finds itself losing reserves, which is practically impossible. At some point, and probably very quickly, one of the banks will feel the pinch of a net reserve loss, and that will make it hesitate, forcing the other banks to abandon the scheme as well.

The overall discipline that this chain-gang behaviour imparts on the system is summed up in Figure 1.

Figure 1   Spending equilibrium: free banking

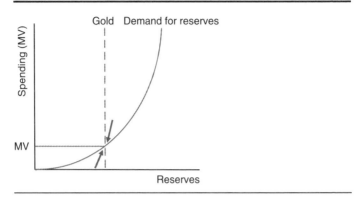

The vertical line in the figure represents the supply of reserves in the Scottish banking system, where reserves consist mainly of gold and silver coin held by the Scottish banks. Those coins must be acquired through the course of trade with other nations. The vertical schedule reflects the fact that their quantity doesn't change with the level of spending within Scotland itself, which is what the figure's vertical axis measures.

The banks' overall demand for reserves is, on the other hand, a function of the value of notes (and perhaps some cheques) being exchanged for goods or services every day, which is to say, on the total amount of spending going on in the Scottish economy. If no one spends anything, the banks don't need any reserves for settlement, because there's nothing to settle! So, the demand schedule starts at the figure's lower left-hand corner.

As spending increases (where the level of spending is equal to the product of the quantity of money in the

Scottish economy and its velocity, and velocity is just how many times each unit of money gets spent in a period of time), the demand for reserves also increases, though generally less than proportionally. Consequently, the demand schedule curves up from the origin. It follows that there's a particular point where the quantity of reserves available is equal to the quantity demanded, and that the system will be in equilibrium at that level of spending.

Now, this equilibrium does not mean that the banks cannot and are not inclined to adjust how big they are and how many IOUs (notes and deposits) they have outstanding. The velocity of money measures how anxious people are to spend money; that is, velocity moves inversely with people's willingness to refrain from spending money, or what economists call their demand for money balances. If velocity declines, people are trying to hold more notes and deposits, and are therefore spending less. In that case the banks – that is, those banks whose notes or deposits are in greater demand – can issue more banknotes and create more deposit credits because the requirement for supply and demand equilibrium allows them to do so. If a particular bank's notes, for example, are being spent less actively, that bank can issue more notes without needing more reserves to cover the presentation of those notes for gold. And, of course, this works in reverse. If the people are spending more aggressively, the banks will find that they had better reduce their outstanding IOUs by lending less.

So, in a free banking system like Scotland's, you have this built-in tendency for spending to be kept very stable. Why is this interesting? It's interesting because many economists today, and especially ones styling themselves 'market monetarists', have been arguing that, if we only could get central banks to maintain stable levels of spending, we would have greater financial stability. Well, in Scotland, such stability, instead of depending on deliberate government 'policy', was the natural result of a competitive currency and banking system.

Figure 2   Quarterly value of Fedwire transactions and nominal GDP (1992 = 100)

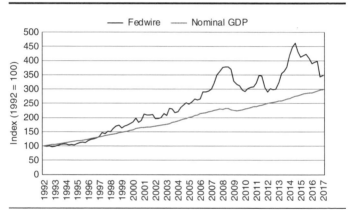

Just to drive home that point, Fedwire handles most of the large-scale ('wholesale') clearing and settlement transactions in the US today. It is a Federal Reserve clearing system. In Figure 2, the jagged line shows what has happened to the total amount of payments through Fedwire over time, over the course of the subprime boom and bust. As you can see, payments increase substantially during the boom, and collapse during the bust. The figure suggests

– though of course it hardly proves – that stability of spending is conducive to overall financial stability.

If instead we had a competitive system that tended to maintain a stable equilibrium of spending relative to reserves, we would have kept to a straight line, or something closer to it. We might have had a lot less turmoil as a result.

Very well, enough about the recent crisis, and about Scotland. Let's talk about England. First of all, I want to remind everyone that early central banks, including the Bank of England, were not set up for the purpose of achieving greater financial stability. They were set up for fiscal reasons. The law establishing the Bank of England was itself a revenue measure.

So, it should not surprise us to discover that the Bank of England, and other early central banks, did not serve to stabilise their economies. In fact, their presence was destabilising. It was so because, instead of participating in a chain-gang-like competitive regulatory process, a privileged central bank ends up becoming a sort of 'Pied Piper' of credit, capable of leading other banks into a general overexpansion of credit, or into a general contraction.

Why is that? It's the consequence of one bank having exclusive privileges. In the case of the Bank of England, those privileges included a monopoly of currency issue at first limited to London and its environs and eventually expanded to all of England and Wales. This privilege forced less privileged banks to stock and reissue the Bank of England's notes instead of issuing their own notes, and thus to regard the Bank of England's notes and other claims against it, and not just gold coin, as cash reserves. Because

Bank of England notes were more convenient than coin, the tendency was for the other English banks to actually send all their gold to the Bank of England in exchange for those notes, or other claims against the Bank of England.

Now let's return to our reserve supply–demand figure to see what effect this has. We start with the system in the equilibrium we considered previously, when gold was the only reserve medium. Now suppose that one bank, the Bank of England, is rewarded a monopoly of currency, and that in response the other banks exchange all their gold for claims against the Bank of England, including its notes. The effective sum of reserves is now no longer just equal to the available gold. It's equal to the amount of IOUs that the central bank chooses to create.

It follows that, by choosing to create more of its own IOUs, the Bank of England can sponsor a general expansion by all the other banks that gain possession of those IOUs. It was owing to the Bank of England's Pied Piper status that England suffered from regular financial crises while Scotland did not. The amount of spending in England would clearly depend on how generous the Bank of England was in credit creation. If it created more credits, it made more reserves available to other English banks and led them all in a general expansion, which would raise total spending. But that increased spending would eventually tend to raise English prices, surely? Basic monetary theory suggests that $MV = Py$, where P is the price level, y is the real output of the economy, M is the monetary base, and V is the velocity at which money circulates. Because real output is independent of total spending in the long run, the tendency would be for more spending to raise prices.

In the context of an international gold standard, if prices in England go up relative to prices elsewhere in the world, an adjustment mechanism first described by David Hume would be set in motion. According to that 'Price-Specie-Flow' mechanism, gold would flow from England to other places where prices haven't been rising because, in gold terms, goods have become relatively cheaper in those other places.

I've now summarised the key ingredients of the classic nineteenth-century and late eighteenth-century English financial boom–bust cycle. Excessive expansion by the Bank of England would lead to a corresponding expansion by the whole English banking system, and thence to rising prices, followed by an outflow of gold from the Bank of England. That outflow would cause the Bank of England to suddenly contract credit to conserve its own reserves and avoid going bankrupt. Finally, the Bank's switch from easy to tight money would put the squeeze on other English banks, plunging the economy into a crisis.

The significant point here is not simply that England, with its monopolistic currency system, was exposed to crises of this type again and again, but that Scotland, despite operating on the same British pound unit, managed to escape the crises from which England suffered. Why was that so? The explanation resides in the difference between the banking systems of the two countries. At least, no one has been able to identify any other reason why Scotland should have escaped England's troubles.

Walter Bagehot and the role of central banks

Walter Bagehot is very important in this story. Bagehot plays a somewhat tragic part in the history of central banking and of financial instability. Bagehot published his famous book, *Lombard Street*, in 1873. In it, Bagehot drove home the necessity of the Bank of England serving as a lender of last resort during crises. Specifically, he argued that, when faced with an external drain of gold, instead of tightening credit, the Bank had a public obligation to lend freely to solvent firms, albeit at a high interest rate.

The tragedy is that Bagehot has since been understood by generations of central bankers to have *recommended* central banks as devices for managing crises. If you don't have a lender of last resort, they now wonder, how are you going to prevent crises?

Yet in *Lombard Street* Bagehot is quite explicit in saying that the ultimate cause of crises in England was the Bank of England's monopoly privileges, which led to the centralisation of gold in its coffers. So far as Bagehot was concerned, this system of centralised reserves at the Bank of England was the root cause of instability. He argued that, if England could have done so, it would have been better off never creating a monopoly bank of issue, and therefore never having promoted the centralisation of reserves that is the inevitable result of such a monopoly. In several passages in *Lombard Street,* and in its closing paragraphs especially, Bagehot makes clear that his lender of last resort advice is only what economists nowadays would call a 'second best' solution:

I know it will be said that in this work I have pointed out a deep malady, and only suggested a superficial remedy. I have tediously insisted that the natural system of banking is that of many banks keeping their own cash reserve, with the penalty of failure before them if they neglect it. I have shown that our system is that of a single bank keeping the whole reserve under no effectual penalty of failure. And yet I propose to retain that system, and only attempt to mend and palliate it.

I can only reply that I propose to retain this system because I am quite sure that it is of no manner of use proposing to alter it … You might as well, or better, try to alter the English monarchy and substitute a republic, as to alter the present constitution of the English money market, founded on the Bank of England, and substitute for it a system in which each bank shall keep its own reserve. There is no force to be found adequate to so vast a reconstruction, and so vast a destruction, and therefore it is useless proposing them.

The sad, indeed tragic, outcome of the distortion of Bagehot's message, which is still being perpetuated by central bankers everywhere, is that his authority has been invoked by those who have since saddled almost every nation on the globe with a central bank. Yet Bagehot himself left no room for doubting that he regarded the best system to be one with competing, independent banks of issue, each holding its own cash reserves, rather than a system in which one bank alone enjoyed the privilege of issuing currency, thanks to which it ended up holding all the gold in the country.

The cause of financial instability in the pre-Federal-Reserve US

I would now like to say a little bit about a different pair of banking and currency systems. I have talked about the difference between England and Scotland. I want to move now from Great Britain to America, to look at the difference between the nineteenth-century monetary systems of the US and Canada.

It is important that I do so because, after all, we had financial crises in the US during the nineteenth century; yet we did not have a central bank until the Fed was established in 1914. Although I believe, like Bagehot, that central banks are inherently destabilising, that doesn't mean that you cannot have financial and economic instability without a central bank. Decentralised monetary systems, if poorly regulated, can also be unstable; and the US is a good example of this.

Although the antebellum US had more than its share of monetary instability, I wish to draw attention to the US financial crises that took place after the Civil War. Those crises had their roots in misguided financial interventions that took place during the war. The common theme between the American and the British stories is, by the way, that when governments tamper with their monetary systems to achieve fiscal ends, stability goes out the window.

During the Civil War, the Union government undertook a number of monetary 'reforms', most of which ultimately proved harmful. Before the war banks were established

and regulated – often badly – by state-government authorities only; and state banks were the only source of circulating currency. One of the Civil War reforms established
a new system of federally chartered banks, the so-called
'national' banks, granting them the right to issue circulating notes provided that the notes were backed by US government securities.

The idea was simple. The Northern government had a
war to pay for. If the new banks it authorised could all be
forced to back their notes with US government securities,
the establishment of such banks would generate revenue
to help pay for the war. To encourage state banks to switch
to national charters, the Northern government eventually imposed a prohibitive 10 per cent tax on all state bank
notes, making a switch compulsory for any bank that
wished, as the vast majority did, to stay in the business of
issuing paper currency. The bond-security requirement
might also make national bank notes safe, so long as the
bonds held their value. While the fortunes of the North
were occasionally in doubt during the war, US bonds were
indeed perfectly safe afterwards.

Yet there was a problem. The new system tied the total
supply of currency to the available supply of government
debt. After the war, the government took advantage of annual budget surpluses to retire its debt. As it did so, there
were fewer and fewer bonds available to secure national
bank notes. Between 1880 and 1890 the supply of national
banknotes fell from almost $350m worth to less than half
that amount! While the stock of currency was rapidly contracting, the US economy was growing no less rapidly.

The post-Civil-War currency system, with its bond-backing requirements, also did not allow for any seasonal adjustment of the supply of currency. There were no peaks at harvest time. Yet it was notorious that, at harvest time, there was a very strong increase in the demand for circulating money relative to bank deposits. The system was utterly incapable of accommodating farmer's requirements for 'moving the crops'.

To repeat: these very serious shortcomings of the pre-Fed currency system were all due to the Civil War attempt to force the banking system to help pay the costs of the war.

I am explaining this because many people will tell you that the Fed was set up in 1914 in response to the shortcomings of *unregulated* banking. Instead, pre-Fed instability was caused, not by a lack of regulation, but by misguided regulation.

The 'inelastic' nature of the pre-Fed US currency system was one of several causes – all traceable to misguided regulations – of a series of severe financial crises, culminating in the notorious panic of 1907. In every case, restrictive currency regulations played a very important role. Restrictions on branch banking were another contributing cause.

A comparison of the US experience with Canada's is extremely revealing, and especially so in light of the frequent claim that the problems of the pre-1914 US system stemmed from the fact that the US lacked a central bank.

If you look at the Canadian money supply during the same pre-1914 period, you will see secular growth in that supply, along with a very clear sawtooth pattern, involving regular spikes in the supply of currency, consistent with the harvest season, from August to September or October.

This pattern of currency supply looks like what we might expect had an all-wise and knowing central bank been managing Canada's currency supply, making sure that it was always just adequate to meet the Canadian economy's fluctuating needs. In fact, although the supply of Canadian currency adjusted as needed, allowing Canada to avoid all the crises from which the US suffered, much as Scotland avoided the crises from which England suffered, central banking had nothing to do with it: Canada didn't establish a central bank until 1935!

Instead, Canada's currency system was modelled on the Scottish system, with many of Canada's banks having been set up by Scottish Canadians. Like Scotland, Canada had numerous banks of issue with nationwide branch networks that were subject to very few regulations.

So we have two sets of banking systems, each involving one unregulated and decentralised banking system and another that was either centralised or heavily regulated or both. Of course, no two countries are alike, so the comparisons aren't perfect: for one thing, Scotland was and remains much smaller than England economically. Canada was and is still much smaller, economically speaking, than the US. And yet, the comparisons are too important to be ignored. Alas, whereas during the nineteenth century many people, including expert economists, were perfectly aware of the differences between these systems, and of the obvious superiority of the free and decentralised systems, for the most part people are no longer aware of the nature and the success of those bygone Scottish and Canadian systems. Certainly, very few US citizens today realise that Canada was crisis free at a time when we were battling with one financial crisis after another.

As you know, despite Canada's example, the US did not choose to deregulate its financial system as a means for correcting that system's shortcomings. Instead, we set up our own central bank, the Fed, in 1914. What you probably don't know is that that solution was chosen only after numerous attempts were made to deregulate the US system, all of which were thwarted by Nelson Aldrich, the Republican Chairman of the Senate Finance Committee, who was under the influence of powerful New York banks and who therefore opposed any reform that threatened those banks' interests. In particular, Aldrich opposed Canadian-style reform, because such reform, by allowing for nationwide branch banking, would have undermined the big New York banks' lucrative correspondent business. (For details see my 2016 Cato Institute *Policy Analysis*, 'New York's Bank'[1].)

Of course, the establishment of the Federal Reserve System did not put an end to US financial crises, as its proponents said it would. To drive home that point, I needn't trouble you with a review of all the serious financial crises by which the US has been afflicted since 1914: your memories of the most recent (2008) crisis should suffice.

---

[1]   https://www.cato.org/publications/policy-analysis/new-yorks-bank-natio nal-monetary-commission-founding-fed

It may nevertheless surprise you to learn that the US economy hasn't even become less unstable since 1914, or even since 1945, than it was before the Federal Reserve was established! According to Christina Romer, one of our more authoritative monetary historians: 'Major real economic indicators have not become dramatically more stable between the pre-World War I and post-World War II eras, and recessions have become only slightly less severe on average'.

Note that Romer wrote this in 1999 – that is, well before the recent crisis. Note as well that her comparison leaves out the period between the two wars. Including that period – which means including three more severe crises, those of 1920–21, 1929–33 and 1936–37 – makes the overall record of stability since 1914 far worse than that for the decades before 1914, which, as we've seen, was itself extremely poor, thanks mainly to misguided regulations.

Throw in the subprime crisis, and the Fed's record becomes still worse. In short, anyone who claims that the Fed's establishment resulted in a definite if delayed reduction in US financial instability is guilty of ignoring what the record actually shows.

Price stability

What about price stability? Would a free banking system automatically achieve it? Not quite. Nor should we want it to! I struggled with the title assigned to my talk because in my view a stable price level or inflation rate is neither desirable nor necessary for overall monetary and macro-economic stability.

The simple reason for that is that the general level of prices can rise or fall for more than one reason and it is very important to distinguish these different reasons.

When central bankers talk about deflation today, they have a tendency to assume that the only way deflation can happen is because spending is collapsing. And of course, if spending is collapsing then that is unfortunate. The decline in prices that happens is itself actually not what is bad. What is bad is the fact that people are spending less and this is not only reflected in falling prices but, more seriously, reflected in declines in output. With less output, you also have less employment.

This is what typically happens in downturns, such as the downturns of 2008–9 or 1936–38 or 1930–33. By the way, in every one of these episodes I have just mentioned, Federal Reserve misconduct played a crucial role.

But in any event, in these episodes of deflation, which are usually relatively short term, demand collapses and therefore there is less spending to purchase goods. As fewer goods are being demanded, less labour will be demanded as well, so unemployment ensues.

But, prices can also fall because there is more output of goods as a result of supply improving, rather than demand suffering a setback. That is quite a different sort of deflation. Here we have more goods being produced at cheaper costs, prices fall to reflect falling costs, but quantities are growing. That is, the quantity demanded and supplied is going up.

Most deflation throughout history, until the twentieth century, was this good sort of deflation. For example, in both the UK and the US, between 1873 and 1896 or so, we had a long stretch of deflation at a mild annual rate of something like 2 per cent.

But, for the most part, that deflation was 'good' deflation. That is, it had nothing to do with collapsing demand, although there were cyclical episodes where demand was collapsing. It was mainly a result of productivity gains from all sorts of technological improvements, which under the gold standard were allowed to be reflected in falling prices because the output of money in the gold standard, though adequate to provide for some kinds of growth such as population growth, allowed prices to fall – at least pending new gold discoveries – in response to improvements in productivity.

There is a myth by the way, still subscribed to by some economists, that the whole period from 1873 to 1896 was another Great Depression – a Great Depression that lasted more than two decades. But they draw that inference simply from the fact that prices were falling and by making the assumption that, if prices were falling, everyone must have been depressed.

Figure 3 is a chart that actually is very revealing about the period I was just talking about. The black line shows an index of prices in the US. They are declining, from an index number of just under 12 down to almost 8. However, the grey line, which shows spending, suggests a different picture. What we want is a stable flow of spending. You can have positive growth in spending, but you want it to be growing steadily.

That is not quite what we had. There were dips around 1870, 1873, 1874 and 1875. Then there is another dip around 1893. Those are the crises I mentioned. In every one of those cases, you had bad deflation as well as good deflation. The bad deflation is related to the collapse of spending. All the rest of the deflation is actually not due to any decline in spending. It is all due to improvements in the availability of goods and to productivity growth. It is all good deflation.

Figure 3   US CPI (average 1982–84 = 100), US nominal GDP (millions of dollars)

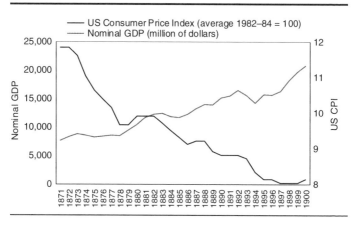

It is stability of spending that is important and stability of spending is consistent with prices tending to fall, if the progress of productivity calls for it. That is what is really desirable for overall macroeconomic and monetary stability.

The alternative fetish of maintaining a stable rate of inflation, without regard to what that implies regarding the pattern of spending, is a cause of a lot of economic trouble.

For example, during the subprime boom, spending was growing very rapidly but eyes were fixed on the inflation rate. American central bank authorities – the monetary authorities – did not see this as a reason to raise interest rates and tighten credit and, as a result, this contributed a lot to the subprime boom.

By contrast, in 2008, when spending began to collapse, still focusing on inflation and particularly on headline inflation, which depended heavily on oil prices, the authorities saw no reason to create more credit and to try to do something that would revive spending. In both cases, they contributed to the overall calamity that was the subprime boom and bust.

As Atkeson and Kehoe suggested in an article in the *American Economic Review* in 2004: 'A broad historical look finds many more periods of deflation with reasonable growth than with depression, and many more periods of depression with inflation than with deflation'. Economists have finally gotten around to discovering that good deflation is very common in the empirical record, but the monetary authorities around the world are still lagging in this understanding and still, therefore, suffer from a price stabilisation or inflation stabilisation fetish which can cause trouble.

It is not, in other words, simply that letting prices fall sometimes is harmless. The problem is that, when central banks prevent prices from falling at those times when productivity improvements suggest that they ought to fall, they can actually create asset bubbles that end up popping. This is extremely important.

Almost any monetary expert you talk to will agree that the prices of *certain things* should get cheaper as their cost of production declines. I cannot imagine an economist saying that there's anything wrong with the price of computers declining over time because we are able to produce them more cheaply. But many of those same economists believe implicitly that, to the extent that we have goods such as computers that are tending to get cheaper, we had better make sure that we have some other goods that get more expensive, or else the price index will decline, and that must mean that we end up depressed!

This sort of thinking is very common in the economics profession, and we really have to struggle to counter it. It is possible, after all, for the vast majority of goods, or for many goods anyway, to be getting cheaper at the same time in terms of their unit cost of production. Why should the price index not fall to reflect that? The only answer is because central banks will not let it. When they won't let the price index fall they destabilise the economy.

Concluding remarks

Once again, it is stability of spending that is really required for macroeconomic stability, not stability of any price index or of the inflation rate. I have argued that a free banking system has a built-in tendency to stabilise spending because of the way the demand for reserves depends on how much spending there is.

In all of this, I share common ground with the market monetarists such as David Beckworth, who is a former student of mine, and Scott Sumner. These fellows have been arguing, I think quite convincingly, that lack of stability of spending contributed to the recent crisis and that central banks should adopt stability of spending as their criterion of overall monetary stability.

Well, we free bankers are a little bit ahead of them because we have always known that. We just happen to think that central banks are poor instruments for implementing this idea and that markets can do it better if you would only let them do so.

In today's economies, of course, we have fiat monies; we do not have gold. We must therefore have some device to artificially constrain the growth of fiat money. Whether you call it a central bank or not is a matter of semantics. But I believe that if we must have some sort of central bank, it should be a stripped-down central bank that simply maintains a stable supply of reserves. If we would then allow our banks to operate free from harmful, restrictive regulations, we could have a free banking system that replicates some of the success of former such systems.

So, we come all the way back to the Scottish case. We can't turn back the clock, of course, and nobody is suggesting that we should. But since I'm often accused of wishing we could, allow me to say that taking advantage of the lessons of history isn't a matter of replicating what unhindered markets did in the past.

It's important nonetheless that we recognise what happened in those countries that had free banking systems in the past. In light of that understanding, we must ask ourselves whether we have been moving down a wrong path for the last century or more. We must wonder whether we have made a mistake by staking our hopes upon more-and-more centralisation and regulation of our monetary systems, instead of relying on competitive markets, as we have done for most other industries, to supply our financial products. Had we gone the other way, following the Scottish example, might we have achieved greater financial stability? Might we have had fewer crises, and a pattern of price-level changes more consistent with under-lying changes in goods' costs of production? Might the world have been one in which anyone could look at a good the price of which had fallen and say: 'Ah, isn't it nice that such-and-such is cheaper to make these days than it used to be?' That's the kind of price stability that really matters, and the kind we should be striving for.

It is only once people understand both the true mean-ing of financial stability, and the capacity of free and competitive financial markets to contribute to its achievement, that we may be able to take the next step, consisting not of any attempt to revive past arrangements, but instead toward the unleashing of a wholly modern system of mar-ket-based financial regulation that is likely to prove even better.

2 QUESTIONS AND DISCUSSION

AUDIENCE MEMBER: As it is a Hayek lecture, let's invoke the Hayekian triangle. You didn't mention capital structure. So, my question is as follows. If we focus on spending and target spending, do you think that this will solve the problem with the Hayek triangle? And if we already have a problem there and the capital structure is wrong, do you think it is not going to work? If we just kept the spending at that level and we already have malinvestment, then the system cannot clean itself. So, can you just throw some light on this?

GEORGE SELGIN: Yes, I can. Well, I can actually answer this question and yet spare myself having to delve into Hayekian triangles and all that, which I have a feeling some people here would rather not know much about, by pointing to the simple fact that Hayek himself thought stable spending was consistent with avoiding trade cycles – not price level stability, but stability of spending.

In *Prices and Production*, in the second edition at least, and in *Monetary Theory and the Trade Cycle*, his two main works on business cycle theory, and in some other essays as well, Hayek explicitly said that what you ideally need is stability. What you need is stability of M*V (the money supply times velocity of circulation), which is exactly the sort of stability that I said a free banking system tends to promote. 'Tends' is a very important word for economists. We realise there is many a source of interference in this tendency, but still.

Hayek favoured stability of M*V. That is, he believed not that the money stock should be constant or stable; not that the price level should be constant or stable; but that spending should be constant or stable with increases in the money stock just compensating for declines in the velocity of money, and vice versa, which means a stable flow of spending.

Now, at the time he was writing, Hayek conceived of stability as absolute stability. That is, he would have spending be constant: or at least he spoke in those terms rather than in terms of a stable growth rate of spending. The difference between those things is perhaps much less important than that you should have one of them rather than one of these phoney criteria of stability being implemented, whether by authorities or by some alternative system.

So, Hayek himself believed it. Let me just say that my own knowledge of the way the Hayekian triangle works is such that I have no confidence in my ability to contradict Hayek on this point, so I will just rely on his authority to answer the question as I have. I hope that's okay.

TIM CONGDON: You had the Scottish banking system with the reserves being gold. Do you want to go back to the gold standard?

GEORGE SELGIN: If I had a magic wand and could restore a standard just like the pre-war gold standard (the post-war versions of the gold standard were all disasters in my opinion), I think I would. I don't think we've had a standard, certainly not an international standard, that has combined overall domestic and exchange rate stability since. It is no coincidence that monetary experts spent much of the post-war period right up through Bretton Woods trying to recreate what had existed before World War I.

Unfortunately, in order to have a magic wand capable of doing that, you would have to have one that would repeal World War I among other things and in fact, for all kinds of reasons, I don't think we can do it. I don't think we can recreate what we had. For one reason, many countries were involved. It is hard enough to get monetary reform of any sort through in one country at a time.

Second and perhaps more importantly, I know of no mechanism by which we could reintroduce a gold standard in any one country, except by having public authorities (monetary authorities) agree to do so by making their own monies once again convertible into gold. It is totally possible for them to do that, but the credibility genie, so to speak, has come out of the central bank bottle and cannot be stuffed back in easily.

We all know how fixed-exchange-rate systems operated by central banks have tended to be subject to speculative attacks and I'm afraid a new gold standard in which a central bank was the responsible party for gold convertibility would be attacked as well. I don't have to tell British people about how nasty speculative attacks on central banks are, particularly those who were around at the time of the so-called snake.

So, I don't think you can do it. Now, you can certainly repeal laws that prevent people privately from spontaneously turning to alternatives whether gold or anything else, but again in that case, they run up against the tremendous advantage of established currencies, fiat currencies, due to what economists call 'network externalities'. Basically, it is hard to use a currency that hardly anybody else uses. It is hard to be early jumping on a new currency bandwagon.

If gold cannot evolve spontaneously just by letting it, if central banks must be part of any process of re-establishing a gold standard, and if central banks themselves are likely to be the victims of speculative attacks by rational people who don't trust them to maintain the standard, a new gold standard reform, even if it could somehow be achieved in just one country, is not likely to survive.

Once again, if only one country does it, particularly if it is not a very large country, it won't have the stability properties of the old gold standard, which depended on the gold standard being an international standard.

That is a long answer to the question which says I love the pre-war gold standard, nobody can convince me central banks will ever do better, but I don't think we can have it again. Therefore, we must work with established fiat monies and try to reform those as best as we can while also giving people the freedom of choice that both Hayek and I think is absolutely desirable. But I don't have Hayek's confidence in how far that freedom will take us in the way of spontaneous monetary reform.

JOHN BUTLER: I work for a company called Goldmoney. We are building a parallel financial infrastructure fully backed by gold that allows for full commerce, business, savings, payments, all of it. Over the past year, we've signed up a million users.

In the same way that Airbnb is breaking down the hotel cartels; in the same way that Uber is breaking down the taxi cartels (that was unthinkable once upon a time, especially in a place like London); in the same way that Amazon years ago started breaking down some of the old retail cartels (and I'm using the word 'cartel' loosely here for effect), could it be that one could spontaneously, from below, break down the monetary cartel through a technology that is democratised in its access to gold? In the same way Uber democratised its access to taxis, Airbnb democratises access to hotels and Amazon has democratised access to really, really big economy of scale retail, why can it not be done with gold? The technology exists.

AUDIENCE MEMBER: My question is on wages. When you have got very stable prices over a long period of time, it could actually imply quite good rises in living standards, even if people's wages aren't increasing. Are people psychologically comfortable with that? Do the historical records show that? Or are people quite psychologically averse to not getting a wage increase for many years, or even an actual nominal wage decrease?

AUDIENCE MEMBER: You mentioned towards the start about how central banks have been brought in to help finance war and also about state control and so on. I would be interested in your thoughts about how we can reform monies in the face of central banking given the fact there is this intrinsic control element that links back to the state and its role in society.

GEORGE SELGIN: Excellent questions. The first one allows me to elaborate a little bit on my claims about getting back to gold spontaneously.

I don't want to be guilty of hubris, which I would be if I were to say we will never be able to get over network tendencies and network effects in order to get to a position where rival private monies displace the established fiat monies. That is why I believe we should have no laws interfering with such efforts.

I also realise that economists can easily underestimate the capacity of clever entrepreneurs just to get over the problems presented by the existence of goods and services that are out there and that seem to have an absolute lock on the marketplace and establish alternatives against all odds. As such, I am all for efforts, like the gentleman's, to try to entrepreneurially overcome the tendency of people to stick with a money that is already in widespread use. I applaud them. I think we cannot count on such efforts to give us monetary reform and I think we had better try to save those fiat monies and make them less perilous than they already are while allowing such efforts to proceed as well. That is what I favour.

So, if a gold standard could prove popular with people once again, if it could take hold privately, spontaneously and, I hope, spread, so that it becomes as widely used as the old gold standard, then I think we could have something like we once had again. But if we rely on governments to do it, we will only give the gold standard a new black eye.

On the issue of whether people will always want wage increases, in my IEA pamphlet *Less Than Zero* I defended what is called a 'productivity norm', because the price level moves inversely with productivity gains. To put it more prosaically, things get cheaper, they cost less, and we allow it to happen.

But, in that system, factor prices (for example, wages) are not allowed to fall. They tend to be stable. That is an extreme productivity norm where you let deflation happen as goods get cheaper. That is as far as anyone wants to go in defending deflation.

Let us take that extreme case. In general, your factor prices are stable. Now, what does it mean to say that they are stable? Let's just assume that it means that wage rates are stable. That does not mean that no one gets a rise. It means that the person doing the same job as you a generation from you makes the same money at the same stage of his career as you do, but you still have a career where you earn more over time as your own productivity improves.

So, it is not the case that a stable wage rate means that the average individual, if you like, cannot look forward to getting rises. It is simply not true. And that is in the extreme case.

Now, the more we allow for some growth over time in nominal spending, 1 per cent, 2 per cent, 3 per cent ... in such a way that growth in spending is more than is necessary to merely maintain a stable wage rate, the more we can provide for wage increases, not just for the typical person over time but across generations. We can do that too if we wish, but I don't think it is absolutely necessary to overcome the problem.

And again, it is a matter of transparency. It is true there will be some people under a productivity norm who don't get rises, but what does that mean? It means they are not any good: they are not earning rises. The only people who earn rises are the people who, over time, become more productive.

When it comes to central banking under the current structure, we need to fall back on imposing some other monetary rules on central banks. Let's remember that the gold standard was, as far as central banks that adhered to it were concerned, a monetary rule.

To be honest, though, the real basis for the success of the gold standard was not the fact that it was a monetary rule, it was the fact that many of the countries involved, including Canada and Scotland but quite a few others as well (the US among them before 1914), did not have central banks.

The gold standard was simply a contractual relationship between banks and their customers. It wasn't a rule, it wasn't a policy. It was: 'You pay me back my gold or you're bust. You're in default. You close up shop'. That is what held the old gold standard together. That is why a gold standard based on modern central banks is going to be a flimsy thing because they don't have to do that. They can say: 'There's no contract. We've changed our mind'.

Still, since we are stuck with central banks, the best we can do is impose some rule on them and ideally do it in such a way that they cannot disobey it with impunity. I don't think imposing a convertibility rule will work because it will be subject to speculative attacks. That is not true of rules like those governing how rapidly money grows or, more importantly, telling a central bank: 'You must maintain a certain level of stability of nominal spending, you must have this target and you must stick to it'.

The ECB's 2 per cent inflation target is a flawed target. A similar target saying that the central bank should maintain 2 per cent nominal GDP growth is a much better target. It is still not good enough.

I favour changing the mechanism that is behind the management of the supply of fiat money so that this sort of result can be implemented automatically without any body of central bankers convening and deciding how to do it on a day-to-day or month-to-month basis.

I want to replace discretionary central banking, not just in the sense of imposing a rule that central bankers should obey, but in the sense of creating a mechanism that automatically implements the rule. Scott Sumner is also working on such a proposal. I think there are a number of ways we could do it.

For shock value, I talk about the doomsday mechanism. I want a doomsday central bank. We set it going to let nominal spending grow at 2 per cent a year and you cannot stop it, ever.

The point is that this creates tremendous credibility and it pins down expectations. The fact that you cannot stop the thing is a virtue. It is not a bug. That is the sort of reform I would favour.

But we should remember that any plan today, even to go back to gold, that involves central banks essentially is a plan to impose some kind of monetary rule. We don't have to be slaves to history. We can think about all the different rules and all the ways of implementing them and come up with what we think is best now. We don't have to try to replicate what we had in the past, even if we think highly of that past arrangement.

3 SELGINIAN FREE BANKING

A commentary on George Selgin's lecture

Kevin Dowd

In his 2016 Hayek lecture, George Selgin makes some great points about the benefits of free banking and on this subject I agree with him one hundred per cent. I agree with him too on related issues, such as Bagehot and the manifestly obvious failures of central banking. I admit that I might be a little biased, however, as I have long been saying similar things myself. I could go on to list the many points where our views coincide, but if I did that, I would end up summarising the first part of his lecture because I agree with all of it.

The fun starts with the second half. In this context I am reminded of an old joke from *Punch* in 1892:

Bishop: 'I'm afraid you've got a bad egg, Mr. Jones.'

Curate: 'Oh, no, my Lord, I assure you that parts of it are excellent.'

Well, the free banking parts were excellent, but I have serious reservations about George Selgin's macroeconomics. There is also a hint of something not being quite right here, as I struggle to understand how his support for free banking is to be reconciled with a macroeconomic perspective that has distinctly Keynesian overtones. As a result, Selginian free banking is a rather strange beast. Indeed, it reminds me of one of those mythical creatures such as a centaur or a mermaid that consists of the halves of two different animals stuck together. Just as there are good reasons why these creatures never actually existed, there are also good reasons to doubt that Selginian free banking would actually work if it were tried. I am not the only one to have this opinion: back in 1992, Leland Yeager carried out a careful analysis of this same issue and concluded (my italics):

> Fiat money managed to satisfy some macroeconomic criterion – ... total or per capita nominal income, a productivity norm, or whatever – *precludes* decentralizing and privatizing the issue of money.

That is the problem in a nutshell.

Free banking and the gold standard: is there an alternative?

Let's go back to basics. To me, there is one natural form of free banking – free banking under a gold standard. We know that this system works well. George explained this in this lecture. We also know why this system worked: it harnessed market discipline under conditions where currency issuers are obliged to redeem their currency for gold or for instruments convertible into gold. Therefore, I agree with him that competitive issue is more stable than monopoly issue. He is clearly correct on these matters.

My concern is that having laid out the evidence convincingly, he did not draw the obvious conclusion – that if that system worked so well then, then surely that same system is the obvious preferred choice now. That system was not some Heath Robinson job in which 'free banking' is superglued onto a discretionary fiat monetary system, but free banking *based on a gold standard*.

This puzzles me because George himself cannot be dismissed as one of the usual aurophobic fiat money crowd who parrot the 'relic of a barbarous age' mantra. It puzzles me more because the historical gold standard has many of the features of which he approves, including the productivity norm. As productivity grows – and one thinks of the late nineteenth-century deflation – prices generally fall, and I agree with him that this deflation is not some bogey to be feared.

So what does George actually advocate in his lecture? Free banking, obviously, but it is not clear (at least not to me) what *type* of free banking system he is supporting. He makes positive comments about the gold standard, regards inflation targeting as a 'fetish' so he presumably does not support that, and makes positive comments about systems to stabilise spending/reserves and about nominal GDP (NGDP) targeting. However, his comments on these issues are vague and one is left with the impression that, macroeconomically, he supports some form of NGDP targeting system.

Let me therefore offer my own perspective and go back to first principles. The first question is: what criteria are we looking for in a good system? I would suggest that we want a rule, as opposed to discretion, although I would go further and suggest that we want a sound monetary standard. So discretion is out. We want financial stability and so central banking and other forms of destabilising state intervention, including a central bank lender-of-last-resort function and government deposit insurance, are out. I would also suggest that we should be looking for tons of evidence that any system we propose would actually work. By this criterion the gold standard is in, and it seems to me that most other proposed schemes, possibly all of them, are out. As for the macroeconomy, we obviously want stability but reasonable people might disagree on what that might entail, for example, stable prices or stable spending. There are also ancillary issues such as short-term versus long-term stability and there are likely trade-offs to be addressed. There are incentive issues too. These include public choice issues and whether policies and regulators create the right or wrong incentives for private sector parties such as risk takers in banks.

I am also mindful of Sir Robert Giffen's famous warning against fancy monetary standards and monetary meddling in general (Giffen 1892):

> For a good money is so very difficult a thing to get, and Governments, when they meddle with money, are so apt to make blunders (and have, in fact, made such blunders without end in the past, of which we have had so many illustrations lately ...), that a nation, which has a good money should beware of its being tampered with, and

especially should beware of any change in the foundation
– the standard for money.

Inferior alternatives to the gold standard

Bearing these points in mind, let us consider some other
possibilities besides free banking on a gold standard. One
is free banking based on a monetary base that is frozen forever. Now George Selgin has done some good work on such
a system, and his analysis of its superior financial stability
properties is convincing. In such a system, prices would
presumably fall as productivity rises. If one had an issue
with this deflation, one might prefer to have the monetary
base grow by $k\%$ a year instead. I suppose too that one
could imagine rule-based systems in which the monetary
base responds in a formulaic way in response, for example,
to NGDP growth or to some other index. However, no such
systems have ever been tried so they all fail the 'tried and
tested' criterion. I also worry about the implications of
such systems for long-term price stability. They involve a
lot of inherent long-term price or inflation-rate risk, which
I believe is both problematic and unnecessary. These reasons suggest to me that all these systems are altogether
too fancy in a Giffenesque sense of the term.

Other proposals such as inflation targeting are worse.
Such systems became fashionable in the decades before the
crisis and their supporters repeatedly assured us that they
would deliver both macroeconomic and financial stability.
Then the crisis hit and it became clear that they had failed

to deliver either, and central bankers now pay their inflation targets little more than lip service. However, the weaknesses of these systems were evident from the start: they gave central bankers way too much discretion to set interest rates, and one thinks of the Greenspan–Bernanke–Yellen put and the series of ever-bigger financial bubbles that those policies produced. There was also little or no sanction to be applied when central banks failed to deliver, especially when the politicians were happy to go with the unconventional monetary policies adopted in response to the crisis.

Then there are the proposals to stabilise NGDP. Most of these proposals simply entail replacing one target, an inflation target, with another target based on NGDP growth. Big deal. Any such system may or may not be better than an inflation-targeting system, but they are, I believe, all forms of managed (and therefore, inevitably, mismanaged) monetary systems. In the standard vanilla variety, an NGDP targeting-system is based on central bank discretion, too. Targets, instruments, indicators. You set your target, say NGDP growth; you choose an indicator; and you set your instrument, presumably, but not necessarily, an interest rate. But whether your instrument is an interest rate or the monetary base, the system still depends on discretion. Going further, Bill Niskanen used to argue that Alan Greenspan was implicitly targeting NGDP and if he is right – and I have no reason to doubt him – then the implication is that NGDP targeting in practice is/was almost indistinguishable from inflation targeting.

NGDP targeting is also rather too Keynesian for my taste, and Keynesianism and free banking do not mix.

While I grant that NGDP targeting has certain short-term stabilising features according to, say, new-Keynesian theory, I am not convinced by that theory. Nor am I persuaded by Hayek's musings on the subject, which have always struck me as vague. There is also an underlying presumption that macroeconomic policy is needed to counter some market failure on the part of the private sector economy. As Joe Salerno (2012) puts it: 'Like any garden-variety Keynesian, Selgin sees these fluctuations in aggregate demand as a market failure that must be offset by Fed policy.' Now I would *not* describe George as a garden-variety Keynesian, but I agree with Salerno's main point. Like him, I don't believe in market failures, except for those caused by failures of government policy, and those are not market failures but *government* failures. Another reason for being sceptical about an NGDP-targeting system is that I have no confidence that anyone can design any NGDP regime that would reliably work in practice or be reliably better than alternatives such as price-level or inflation targeting. Proposals for NGDP targeting are just more examples of blackboard economics. My fear is that, if implemented, NGDP targeting would be as counterproductive as previous attempts to use macroeconomic policy to stabilise the economy. They did not succeed in the past and I see little reason to expect them to succeed now. To quote a classic passage on this subject from Milton Friedman (1960: 9):

> The Great Depression did much to instil and reinforce the now widely held view that inherent instability of a private market economy has been responsible for the major

periods of economic distress experienced by the United States. On this view, only a vigilant government, offsetting continuously the vagaries of the private economy, has prevented or can prevent such periods of instability. As I read the historical record, I draw almost the opposite conclusion. In almost every instance, major instability in the United States has been produced or, at the very least, greatly intensified by monetary instability. Monetary instability in its turn has generally arisen either from governmental intervention or from controversy about what government monetary policy should be. The failure of government to provide a stable monetary framework has thus been a major if not the major factor accounting for our really severe inflations and depressions. Perhaps the most remarkable feature of the record is the adaptability and flexibility that the private market economy has so frequently shown under such extreme provocation.

I regard it as self-evident that monetary policy attempts to stabilise the economy have not improved since Friedman wrote those words nearly 60 years ago.

So let us learn this lesson once and for all: stop trying to manage aggregate demand to counter the cycle. The best counter-cyclical policy is none.

Now *pace* the 'NGDPers', I acknowledge the big run-up in spending in the years prior to the global financial crisis. However, the main factors contributing to this spending boom were (and I am thinking mainly of the US here) the policies of Bernanke et al. in underpinning investment markets using monetary policy, the government's counterproductive attempts to boost the subprime mortgage market, an inadequate bank capital regulatory system that allowed bankers to decapitalise their banks and, underlying these, the financial sector's capture of the regulatory and policy-making apparatus. These all led to policies that promoted a self-serving, short-termist boom–bust cycle and broke the banking system. The spending crash afterwards was then to be expected. These are the real underlying structural problems that need to be fixed and attempts to stabilise aggregate spending do not address these problems or even attempt to do so. The best that monetary policy can be expected to do is to provide a stable framework with reasonable interest rates, and the decade since the financial crisis, including the use of quantitative easing shows that central bankers cannot deliver on even those modest objectives. Am I saying that central bankers were wrong to seek to apply some monetary relaxation as spending crashed? No, but based on the evidence I see, there was no case for there having been anything more on the monetary policy front than some moderate monetary easing and some liquidity support based on high-quality collateral. On the banking policy front, there was (and still is) a need to put down the zombies and recapitalise the banking system.

Finally, one of the best arguments I have come across against NGDP targeting is the following from a well-known expert in the US:

Even if the Fed were somehow legally committed to target NGDP, or some other broad spending measure, from now on, and even if the measure were itself reliable, it wouldn't solve our monetary troubles. And that's because the monetary system itself is dysfunctional, and severely so. If it weren't, it wouldn't take more than $4.5 trillion in Fed assets to keep spending going at a reasonable clip. The defects are partly traceable to policies – including some of the Fed's own – that discourage banks from making certain kinds of worthwhile loans, while encouraging them to hold massive excess reserves.

It's owing to the crippled state of our monetary system, and not to any ambiguity in relevant indicators, that I myself have grave doubts concerning the gains to be expected from further Fed easing, or even from implementing a strict NGDP targeting rule, under present conditions. For if the experience of the last several years is any guide, it may require still more massive additions to the Fed's balance sheet to achieve even very modest improvements in spending; and an NGDP based monetary rule that would serve as a license for the Fed to become a still greater behemoth would not be my idea of an improvement upon the status quo ... Which means that the level of spending is, after all, not the only relevant indicator of whether the Fed is or isn't going in the right direction. Another is the real size of the Fed's balance sheet relative to that of the economy as a whole, which measures the extent to which our central bank is commandeering savings that might otherwise be more productively employed. Other things equal, the smaller that ratio, the better.

And there, folks, is the rub. If you want to know the real dilemma facing the FOMC [Federal Open Market

Committee], forget about the CPI, oil prices, and last quarter's weather. Here's the real McCoy: NGDP growth is too low. But the Fed is too darn big.

And who wrote these words of wisdom? By George, it's George!

You can now see my problem. He makes great points about the benefits of free banking and offers some trenchant criticisms of alternatives to it. But it seems to me that he then goes on to spoil it rather by attempting some reconciliation that is part free banking and part its incompatible opposite, central banking – and activist central banking at that. Or to put it this way, the second half of his talk endorses systems that have either not been tried or have been tried and failed, and I can't work out why he does not prefer the gold-based free-banking systems that are the main evidence base of the successful free banking systems that were the theme of the first half of his talk.[1]

So it's a case of the curate's egg. When he was good, he was very, very good, but when he was not, he was florid.

References

Friedman, M. (1960) *A Program for Monetary Stability*. New York: Fordham University Press.

---

1   George Selgin's position on the gold standard is, however, a nuanced one: he would be happy with a pre-World War I gold standard if it could be resurrected. But, for all sorts of reasons that seem unduly pessimistic to me, he believes that it is not possible. On this subject, I refer the reader to the Q&A after the lecture where this subject was raised.

Giffen, R. (1892) Fancy monetary standards. *Economic Journal* 2(7): 463–71.

Salerno, J. (2012) The Selgin story. Mises Institute blog, 11 July.

Selgin, G. (2015) None of the Fed's business. *Alt-M*, 30 April.

Yeager, L. B. (1992) Toward forecast-free monetary institutions. *Cato Journal* 12(1): Spring–Summer.

4 ON CHAIN GANGS IN FINANCIAL STABILITY

A commentary on George Selgin's lecture

Mathieu Bédard

In his lecture, Professor Selgin compares the market discipline of systems of multiple banks of issue with a chain gang. If one bank were to lend too much money, and act in a way that increased inflation, it would soon be stopped by the other banks, which would drain its reserves – much like a lone prisoner would soon trip and fall trying to run for it while chained to the rest. Even trying to coordinate all prisoners, or in our case banks, to 'run' simultaneously would be very difficult, since the first bank to 'slow down' would drain others of their precious reserves.

Running and chain-gang analogies are sometimes used elsewhere when discussing banking stability. They can be used to describe bank runs, one of the greatest fears associated with unregulated 'free' banking, as well as systemic risk and herd-like behaviour. This comment will explore these other types of chain gang in financial stability, inspired by Professor Selgin's lecture and an extensive bibliography on banking and monetary stability. It is in this spirit that this comment reviews a few chain-gang theories of banking crises.

Systemic risk as a chain-gang effect

One of the greatest, and latest, chain-gang theories of banking crises is systemic risk. This has been compared with nuclear explosions in the press (Kay 2013). It is, at its core, a reformulation of the basic 'too big to fail' intuition. It posits that some banks, or sometimes nearly all banks,[1] should they be allowed to fail, would pose a threat to the whole system. This theory is the ultimate chain gang of banking financial stability: one failure of a systemically important bank would trigger failures at otherwise perfectly sound banks, until the contagion has bankrupted all banks. The chain gang stays together, but they all fail together.

The problem with this theory is that, to put it mildly, it is a struggle to find empirical evidence to validate it. Jeffrey Lacker (1998: 1–2), an economist who would become the president of the Federal Reserve Bank of Richmond, wrote:

In economics, as in any empirical science, the advancement of knowledge essentially falls in one of two categories. At times, some noteworthy phenomenon is observed empirically, and we seek plausible models which display the same phenomenon. If our catalogue of models does

---

1   In fact, in the US pretty much every bank is too big to let its creditors fail. From the creation of the Federal Deposit Insurance Corporation and up until the FDIC Improvement Act of 1991, almost no debtors have suffered any loss, except for two brief periods in the 1980s where the FDIC had become wary of disrupting market discipline (Kaufman 2004). Since 1991, banks' unsecured and uninsured creditor losses are partly shared with the FDIC.

not contain one that displays the observed phenomenon, then we try to construct models that do. On the other hand, sometimes we find that a particular model in our catalogue displays an unusual or remarkable phenomenon. In this case, we go looking for empirical evidence of that the phenomenon [sic] actually occurs in real life.

Systemic risk [...] falls in neither category. The authors report that we do not have any serious models that can be said to display systemic risk, as they define it. Thus systemic risk is not a theoretical phenomenon in search of empirical confirmation. Furthermore, we do not have any convincing empirical evidence of phenomenon [sic] that can be readily identified as systemic risk, and that cannot be explained adequately by existing models in our catalogue. Thus, systemic risk does not appear to be an empirical phenomenon in search of a theoretical explanation either. About the only evidence we have for systemic risk is that many central bank officials speak of it when discussing their lender of last resort function or the risk containment measures they impose on private settlement arrangements.

His words are still valid today, despite the crisis of autumn 2008 and advances in economic research since then.[2] Even the 2008 failure of Lehman Brothers failed to create the kind of systemic risk effect of which central bankers warn. As

2 Do note, however, that systemic risk as Lacker conceived it in this early text was financial contagion. This is now thought to be one of the many components of systemic risk. This does not affect the validity and current relevance of his remarks.

demonstrated by Helwege (2010), out of Lehman Brother's $600 billion of unsecured debt, the largest creditor was the Japanese bank Aozora with $463 million dollars, a sum insufficient to threaten its $7.4 billion dollars of equity.

Chain gangs in asset markets

One of the ways systemic risk would affect other banks, or, if you will, that the next chained prisoner would trip and fall, is illustrated by a comparison of actors in financial markets with lemmings, or to a flock of sheep. These comparisons are used as much to describe financial bubbles as they are used to describe crises. According to these theories, opinions of one person are chained to the opinions of others because, in a crisis setting, it can become rational to ignore one's own private information and instead follow the actions of others (Drehmann et al. 2005). This is sometimes referred to as an informational cascade, because in those situations, as the theory goes, no new information is being created.

The idea of an informational cascade is particularly used when the logic of bank runs is taken out of its original context to describe depositors and also to explain rapid movements on financial markets, such as fire sales. These can happen when many financial companies sell some assets rapidly because they need liquidity to satisfy depositors and other creditors. The value of the assets can then become lower than their long-term, non-crisis value. These pressures can, in and of themselves, reduce significantly the value of other companies that hold these assets.

Two things can be said about this form of chain-gang behaviour. The first is that costs ramp up simultaneously as these preferences are adopted. Costs should provide counter incentives to adopt the herd view, and possibly neutralise them. In fact, it might not matter much whether prices of assets are influenced by herd behaviour or not, because herd behaviour is influenced by the price of assets. In fact price movements should eliminate these behaviours once they are too costly (Avery and Zemsky 1998).

In other words, herd behaviour chain gangs exist when expectations about other people's expectations affect behaviour in the absence of a price system. Once you introduce a coordination mechanism, such as the price system, and profits and losses, these chain gangs disappear.

It is also worth noting that government intervention often causes herd behaviour rather than ameliorates it. Big players such as central banks and financial market authorities pursue policies that explicitly aim to modify, influence and steer price signals (Koppl 2002; Koppl and Yeager 1996; Butos and Koppl 1999).[3] These typically create new arbitrage opportunities, and the harmony of interest is influenced and disconnected from the underlying economic reality. They create a certain type of herd behaviour themselves as investors behave in similar but unpredictable ways to signals from government institutions instead

---

3 Big players can also be any other large entity, private or governmental, that by virtue of its size is insulated from the consequences of its actions. These big players are generally governmental bodies and, of course, government action in the banking markets has encouraged consolidation and the creation of larger institutions in the private sector.

of relying on diverse interpretations of disparate information within markets.

The arbitrage opportunities being pursued are then those created by big players. Because the actions creating those opportunities come from a limited set of players, rather than emerging from all of the market and its millions of actors, they are by definition less predictable. They make the market more volatile. To seek financial stability and less herd behaviour through government intervention in financial markets is, in this sense, paradoxical.

Chain gangs and bank runs

When it comes to bank runs, it is widely thought that rational responses to incentives are the cause of the coordinated behaviour that leads to a run. If a sufficient number of depositors withdraw their deposits at the same time, the bank may become insolvent. The bank fails because it has largely invested the money that is entrusted to it and because liquidating investments quickly is costly. It is a kind of chain gang because if everybody withdraws their money from the bank in a coordinated way, there will not be anything left for the last few in line. There are strong incentives to be among the first few to rush to the bank, creating the crisis in the process – everybody has little to lose and much to gain from being first in line.

This theory of banking crises has been formalised into economic models, the most famous being the article by Diamond and Dybvig (1983), which has become the canonical model of bank runs. It is the 48th most cited article based on the online economic paper archival service RePEc.[4] In a special issue of the *FRB Richmond Economic Quarterly* dedicated to this model, Prescott (2010: 1) described it as 'a workhorse of banking research over the last 25 years and during the recent financial crisis it has been one that researchers and policymakers consistently turn to when interpreting financial market phenomena.' It has in fact become the key model for rationalising banking and financial market problems.

The basic features of this model are still present in most publications on financial stability to this day. The model suggests that banks are inherently unstable; always on the verge of suffering a 'redemption run' at any unrelated 'sunspot'; that it is absolutely necessary that bank runs be suppressed; and that deposit insurance is the most effective way to supresss them. In their model, if banks are to survive it has to be through intervention in the financial system.

Although this intuition might sound so simple and straightforward that it could be a tautology, economic history suggests that it is quite otherwise.

In his lecture, Professor Selgin discusses the American banking system following the Civil War and before the advent of the Federal Reserve and how this era was rife with banking crises. Gorton (1988) studies this era and finds that, in each of the seven crises he identifies, bank runs were the result of a previous event which had suggested a possible depreciation of banking assets. In other

---

4   https://ideas.repec.org/top/top.item.nbcites.html

words, people were not rushing to the bank to withdraw their money from a perfectly sound bank, causing in the process its illiquidity and insolvency. The run on the banks happened because they had made bad investments. This changes the focus because it suggests that banking crises are not a ubiquitous risk associated with the very nature of banking but that they are simply associated with bad investment decisions.[5]

Likewise, Calomiris and Gorton (1991) find that in the period 1875–1913 all banking panics (i.e. a generalised run on all banks) happened within the quarter following an abrupt increase in business failures. Mishkin (1991) studies bank panics from 1857 to 1988, and finds that for all but that of 1873, panics occur well after the recession has started – they are not the cause of the economic slowdown.

Secondly, banks that do go bankrupt because of a bank run are those that are insolvent before the run. Banks that are solvent can generally borrow from other banks and other institutions (historically, clearing houses) and have a large repertoire of possible solutions to help them in a crisis. While bank runs and associated liquidity problems can be aggravating factors, even in the worst bank panic episodes they are causes of bank failure only in exceptional circumstances (Kaufman 1987, 1988). Even in the most fruitful historical era in terms of banking panics and runs, the American National Banking Era, runs were a primary cause of failure in only one

---

5   In this case, as in many others, the bad investments were being influenced by policy, as described by Professor Selgin. Elsewhere, this has been called the legal restriction theory of bank crises (Selgin 1994).

case out of 594 bank bankruptcies (Calomiris and Gorton 1991: 154). Calomiris and Mason (1997) study the banking panic of June 1932 in Chicago and find that no pre-run solvent banks failed. Reviewing this literature, Benston and Kaufman (1995: 225) conclude that 'the policy implications of the Diamond & Dybvig (1983) model are not very useful for understanding the workings of the extant banking and payments system.'

If Diamond and Dybvig (1983) are correct, it should apply to all fractional-reserve banking systems without deposit insurance. But, as evidenced by the US-centric literature cited here, bank runs are much more common in US history than elsewhere, and bank panics are specific to the American National Banking Era and attributable to bank regulation during that era, such as the ban on branch banking that made mergers with insolvent banks impossible, and the bond deposit system that limited emission at a critical time. Bordo (1990: 24) compares bank panics internationally and comments that 'the difference in the incidence of panics is striking.' While over the 1870–1933 period the US had four panics, there were none in Britain, France, Germany, Sweden and Canada despite the fact that 'the quantitative variables move similarly during severe recessions to those displayed here for the U.S.' Table 2-1 in Schwartz (1988: 38–39) reports that from 1790 to 1927 the US experienced fourteen panics, while Britain, the only other country with as many observations, experienced eight, all of them before 1867.

Finally, most runs have in fact been partial 'verification' runs. Depositors eventually figure out that the bank will probably survive and then the crisis and the runs stop. This is impossible in the Diamond and Dybvig (1983) framework: once initiated the run must always go through and make the bank fail. Ó Gráda and White (2003) study a single bank from the 1850s. They investigate depositor behaviour through individual account data, and particularly through the panics of 1854 and 1857. The bank survived both. They find that runs are not sudden, but involve a learning mechanism where random beliefs are progressively dropped, while behaviour motivated by legitimate signals becomes more important over time. Panic does not displace learning in the market processes of bank runs.

Another way to say this is that depositors are not chained to one another. When a few move, the others do not have to move with them.

A reinterpretation

What is common to all of these chain-gang theories is that they view the market reaction to crises as negative, and something to be suppressed by government intervention. It is, however, possible to view these chain gangs under a positive light, much like Professor Selgin views positively the fact that banks are constrained by each other in systems of multiple banks of issue.

Banks, for instance, voluntarily offer a deposit contract that exposes them to the risk of bank runs. While the theoretical literature on banking is full of suggestions to ensure that deposit contracts are run-proof, deposit contracts are still done more or less the same way they have always been done.

One of the reasons for this might be that banks voluntarily choose these types of contract because it lowers their costs by supplying clients with the means to cast a vote of no confidence. If some depositors disagree with the way a bank is being run or are worried about the financial situation at a particular bank, basic deposit contracts make it easy to switch banks, take your money elsewhere, and possibly even change it into another currency.

Thinking about bank runs in terms of votes of no confidence opens the door to the idea that bank runs might even be salutary (White 1999: 122). They close insolvent banks immediately, before its managers have time to squander further wealth. When companies are near to insolvency, the incentives its managers face shift, as they are tempted to take bigger risks in a bet to become solvent again ('gambling for resurrection'). In one extreme case of incentives being distorted by looming financial distress, this idea of a bet took on a literal meaning, as the owners of a paving company took all the money left in their corporate bank account and embarked on a gambling trip to Las Vegas.[6] Bank runs can be thought of as a market response to these situations as they are a 'crowdsourced' way of monitoring bank managers' behaviour and, during financial crises, they filter out solvent banks from insolvent banks, precipitating bank failures before losses to depositors and other creditors can accrue.

---

6   United States Bankruptcy Court, *Matter of Tri-State Paving, Inc.,* W.D. Pennsylvania, 1982.

Of course, this isn't to say that bank runs are efficient, or even optimal. As Kaufman (1987: 21) puts it: '[t]hey did a dirty job in maintaining market discipline, but someone had to do it.' Bank runs are and will always remain costly. But, given the Scottish experience with the Ayr Bank, described by Professor Selgin in his lecture, they cannot be more costly than the spectacular bailouts and too-big-to-fail policies of 2008 and beyond.

Conclusion

The analogy of chain gangs can be used in many senses when it comes to the analysis of banking systems. As George Selgin discussed in the lecture, the discipline of markets in a free banking system creates a chain gang whereby banks have to keep in step. If one makes too many loans and creates too much money, it will eventually empty its own reserves. It is a virtuous chain gang, and we have historical evidence that it exists.

As far as the other suggested chain gangs of coordinated behaviour or situations where all banks tend to behave in a similar, damaging way are concerned, while there is no shortage of literature asserting their existence, there is little empirical evidence. And there is good reason for this.

It is, though, worth mentioning a final type of chain gang – that of coordinated behaviour by government regulators. Governments throughout the world are adopting the same policies with regard to financial stability. The new European bank failure resolution framework, for instance, is largely inspired by the American system. When the US adopted the Financial Stability Oversight Council, with a battery of new powers, Europe quickly created a copycat institution, putting in place stress tests based on the Federal Reserve's model. Deposit insurance, despite a relatively negative opinion from economists, is now present in 59 per cent of the countries studied by Demirgüç-Kunt et al. (2014: 11), up from 44 per cent of countries in 2003. Bank runs, as we have seen, contain the seeds of their own resolution. The problem with coordinated approaches to regulation on the other hand, is that, if governments get things wrong, the whole worldwide banking system could be brought to its knees.

George Selgin's lecture was a timely and important reminder of the self-regulating properties of markets, especially in the banking sector. In much of the prevailing orthodoxy, the lessons from that era have been forgotten or ignored. Instead, we are making the banking system much more dangerous by more and more government control. As George Selgin shows, the empirical evidence is very clear and Selgin's Hayek lecture does a great service by presenting it so lucidly.

References

Avery, C. and Zemsky, P. (1998) Multidimensional uncertainty and herd behavior in financial markets. *The American Economic Review* 88(4): 724–48.

Benston, G. J. and Kaufman, G. G. (1995) Is the banking and payments system fragile? *Journal of Financial Services Research* 9(3–4): 209–40.

Bordo, M. D. (1990) The lender of last resort: alternative views and historical experience. *FRB Richmond Economic Review* 76(1): 18–29.

Butos, W. N. and Koppl, R. (1999) Hayek and Kirzner at the Keynesian beauty contest. *Journal des Économistes et des Études Humaines* 9(2–3): 257–75.

Calomiris, C. W. and Gorton, G. (1991) The origins of banking panics: models, facts, and bank regulation. In *Financial Markets and Financial Crises* (ed. R. Glenn Hubbard), pp. 109–74. University of Chicago Press.

Calomiris, C. W. and Mason, J. R. (1997) Contagion and bank failures during the Great Depression: the June 1932 Chicago banking panic. *The American Economic Review* 87(5): 863–83.

Demirgüç-Kunt, A., Kane, E. J. and Laeven, L. (2014) *Deposit Insurance Database*, Working Paper 14/118, July. Washington, DC: World Bank.

Diamond, D. W. and Dybvig, P. H. (1983) Bank runs, deposit insurance, and liquidity. *Journal of Political Economy* 91(3): 401–19.

Drehmann, M., Oechssler, J. and Roider, A. (2005) Herding and contrarian behavior in financial markets: an internet experiment. *The American Economic Review* 95(5): 1403–26.

Gorton, G. (1988) Banking panics and business cycles. *Oxford Economic Papers* 40(4): 751–81.

Helwege, J. (2010) Financial firm bankruptcy and systemic risk. *Journal of International Financial Markets, Institutions and Money* 20(1): 1–12.

Kaufman, G. G. (1987) The truth about bank runs. In *The Financial Services Revolution: Policy Directions for the Future* (ed. C. England and T. F. Huertas), pp. 9–40. Boston: Kluwer Academic Publishers / Cato Institute.

Kaufman, G. G. (1988) Bank runs: causes, benefits, and costs. *Cato Journal* 7(3): 559–87.

Kaufman, G. G. (2004) Too big to fail in U.S. banking: quo vadis? In *Too Big to Fail: Policies and Practices in Government Bailouts* (ed. B. E. Gup), pp. 153–68. Westport: Praeger.

Kay, J. (2013) The design flaws that lead to financial explosions. *Financial Times*, 12 November.

Koppl, R. (2002) *Big Players and the Economic Theory of Expectations*. Basingstoke: Palgrave Macmillan.

Koppl, R. and Yeager, L. B. (1996) Big players and herding in asset markets: the case of the Russian ruble. *Explorations in Economic History* 33(3): 367–83.

Lacker, J. M. (1998) On systemic risk. Comments presented at the Second Joint Central Bank Research Conference on Risk Measurement and Systemic Risk at the Bank of Japan, Tokyo, 16–17 November.

Mishkin, F. S. (1991) Asymmetric information and financial crises: a historical perspective. In *Financial Markets and Financial Crises* (ed. R. Glenn Hubbard), pp. 69–108. University of Chicago Press.

Ó Gráda, C. and White, E. N. (2003) The panics of 1854 and 1857: a view from the emigrant industrial savings bank. *Journal of Economic History* 63(1): 213–40.

Prescott, E. S. (2010) Introduction to the special issue on the Diamond–Dybvig model. *FRB Richmond Economic Quarterly* 96(1): 1–9.

Schwartz, A. J. (1988) Financial stability and the Federal Safety Act. In *Restructuring Banking and Financial Services in America* (ed. W. S. Haraf and R. M. Kushmeider), pp. 34–62. Washington, DC: American Enterprise Institute.

Selgin, G. A. (1994) Are banking crises free-market phenomena? *Critical Review* 8(4): 591–608.

White, L. H. (1999) *The Theory of Monetary Institutions*. Malden, MA: Blackwell.

ABOUT THE IEA

The Institute is a research and educational charity (No. CC 235 351), limited by guarantee. Its mission is to improve understanding of the fundamental institutions of a free society by analysing and expounding the role of markets in solving economic and social problems.

The IEA achieves its mission by:

- a high-quality publishing programme
- conferences, seminars, lectures and other events
- outreach to school and college students
- brokering media introductions and appearances

The IEA, which was established in 1955 by the late Sir Antony Fisher, is an educational charity, not a political organisation. It is independent of any political party or group and does not carry on activities intended to affect support for any political party or candidate in any election or referendum, or at any other time. It is financed by sales of publications, conference fees and voluntary donations.

In addition to its main series of publications, the IEA also publishes (jointly with the University of Buckingham), *Economic Affairs*.

The IEA is aided in its work by a distinguished international Academic Advisory Council and an eminent panel of Honorary Fellows. Together with other academics, they review prospective IEA publications, their comments being passed on anonymously to authors. All IEA papers are therefore subject to the same rigorous independent refereeing process as used by leading academic journals.

IEA publications enjoy widespread classroom use and course adoptions in schools and universities. They are also sold throughout the world and often translated/reprinted.

Since 1974 the IEA has helped to create a worldwide network of 100 similar institutions in over 70 countries. They are all independent but share the IEA's mission.

Views expressed in the IEA's publications are those of the authors, not those of the Institute (which has no corporate view), its Managing Trustees, Academic Advisory Council members or senior staff.

Members of the Institute's Academic Advisory Council, Honorary Fellows, Trustees and Staff are listed on the following page.

The Institute gratefully acknowledges financial support for its publications programme and other work from a generous benefaction by the late Professor Ronald Coase.

Other books recently published by the IEA include:

From Crisis to Confidence – Macroeconomics after the Crash
Roger Koppl
Hobart Paper 175; ISBN 978-0-255-36693-9; £12.50

Advertising in a Free Society
Ralph Harris and Arthur Seldon
With an introduction by Christopher Snowdon
Hobart Paper 176; ISBN 978-0-255-36696-0; £12.50

Selfishness, Greed and Capitalism: Debunking Myths about the Free Market
Christopher Snowdon
Hobart Paper 177; ISBN 978-0-255-36677-9; £12.50

Waging the War of Ideas
John Blundell
Occasional Paper 131; ISBN 978-0-255-36684-7; £12.50

Brexit: Directions for Britain Outside the EU
Ralph Buckle, Tim Hewish, John C. Hulsman, Iain Mansfield and Robert Oulds
Hobart Paperback 178; ISBN 978-0-255-36681-6; £12.50

Flaws and Ceilings – Price Controls and the Damage They Cause
Edited by Christopher Coyne and Rachel Coyne
Hobart Paperback 179; ISBN 978-0-255-36701-1; £12.50

Scandinavian Unexceptionalism: Culture, Markets and the Failure of Third-Way Socialism
Nima Sanandaji
Readings in Political Economy 1; ISBN 978-0-255-36704-2; £10.00

Classical Liberalism – A Primer
Eamonn Butler
Readings in Political Economy 2; ISBN 978-0-255-36707-3; £10.00

Federal Britain: The Case for Decentralisation
Philip Booth
Readings in Political Economy 3; ISBN 978-0-255-36713-4; £10.00

Forever Contemporary: The Economics of Ronald Coase
Edited by Cento Veljanovski
Readings in Political Economy 4; ISBN 978-0-255-36710-3; £15.00

Power Cut? How the EU Is Pulling the Plug on Electricity Markets
Carlo Stagnaro
Hobart Paperback 180; ISBN 978-0-255-36716-5; £10.00

Policy Stability and Economic Growth – Lessons from the Great Recession
John B. Taylor
Readings in Political Economy 5; ISBN 978-0-255-36719-6; £7.50

Breaking Up Is Hard To Do: Britain and Europe's Dysfunctional Relationship
Edited by Patrick Minford and J. R. Shackleton
Hobart Paperback 181; ISBN 978-0-255-36722-6; £15.00

In Focus: The Case for Privatising the BBC
Edited by Philip Booth
Hobart Paperback 182; ISBN 978-0-255-36725-7; £12.50

Islamic Foundations of a Free Society
Edited by Nouh El Harmouzi and Linda Whetstone
Hobart Paperback 183; ISBN 978-0-255-36728-8; £12.50

The Economics of International Development: Foreign Aid versus Freedom for the World's Poor
William Easterly
Readings in Political Economy 6; ISBN 978–0–255–36731–8; £7.50

Taxation, Government Spending and Economic Growth
Edited by Philip Booth
Hobart Paperback 184; ISBN 978–0–255–36734–9; £15.00

Universal Healthcare without the NHS: Towards a Patient-Centred Health System
Kristian Niemietz
Hobart Paperback 185; ISBN 978–0–255–36737–0; £10.00

Sea Change: How Markets and Property Rights Could Transform the Fishing Industry
Edited by Richard Wellings
Readings in Political Economy 7; ISBN 978–0–255–36740-0; £10.00

Working to Rule: The Damaging Economics of UK Employment Regulation
J. R. Shackleton
Hobart Paperback 186; ISBN 978-0-255-36743-1; £15.00

Education, War and Peace: The Surprising Success of Private Schools in War-Torn Countries
James Tooley and David Longfield
ISBN 978-0-255-36746-2; £10.00

Killjoys: A Critique of Paternalism
Christopher Snowdon
ISBN 978-0-255-36749-3; £12.50

Other IEA publications

Comprehensive information on other publications and the wider work of the IEA can be found at www.iea.org.uk. To order any publication please see below.

Personal customers

Orders from personal customers should be directed to the IEA:

Clare Rusbridge
IEA
2 Lord North Street
FREEPOST LON10168
London SW1P 3YZ
Tel: 020 7799 8907. Fax: 020 7799 2137
Email: sales@iea.org.uk

Trade customers

All orders from the book trade should be directed to the IEA's distributor:

NBN International (IEA Orders)
Orders Dept.
NBN International
10 Thornbury Road
Plymouth PL6 7PP
Tel: 01752 202301, Fax: 01752 202333
Email: orders@nbninternational.com

IEA subscriptions

The IEA also offers a subscription service to its publications. For a single annual payment (currently £42.00 in the UK), subscribers receive every monograph the IEA publishes. For more information please contact:

Clare Rusbridge
Subscriptions
IEA
2 Lord North Street
FREEPOST LON10168
London SW1P 3YZ
Tel: 020 7799 8907, Fax: 020 7799 2137
Email: crusbridge@iea.org.uk